THE OLYMPICS

ANCIENT OLYMPIC GAMES

HAYDN MIDDLETON

Heinemann
LIBRARY

First published in Great Britain by Heinemann Library,
Halley Court, Jordan Hill, Oxford OX2 8EJ,
a division of Reed Educational and Professional Publishing Ltd.
Heinemann is a registered trademark of Reed Educational & Professional Publishing Limited.

OXFORD MELBOURNE AUCKLAND
JOHANNESBURG BLANTYRE GABORONE
IBADAN PORTSMOUTH NH (USA) CHICAGO

Designed by AMR
Illustrations by Art Construction
Originated by Dot Gradations
Printed in Hong Kong/China

03 02 01 00
10 9 8 7 6 5 4 3 2

ISBN 0 431 05918 7

British Library Cataloguing in Publication Data
Middleton, Haydn
 Ancient olympic games. – (The olympics)
 1.Olympic games (Ancient) – Juvenile literature 2.Greece –
 Civilization – Juvenile literature
 1.Title.
 796.4·8·0938

Acknowledgements
The Publishers would like to thank the following for permission to reproduce photographs:
AKG London: E Lessing p13; Allsport: p8; Ancient Art and Architecture Collection Ltd: pp6,
7, 10, 11, 12, 19, 23, 25; Ashmolean Museum, Oxford: p20; British Museum: p17; Colorsport:
p29; Corbis: Tempsport p4; C M Dixon: pp14, 18, 24; Mary Evans Picture Library: p28; Hirmer
Fotoarchiv: p22; Michael Holford: pp15, 17, 21; Kobal Collection: p26; Scala: Galleria
Borghese p27.

Cover photograph reproduced with permission of Ancient Art and Architecture Collection Ltd

Every effort has been made to contact copyright holders of any material reproduced in this
book. Any omissions will be rectified in subsequent printings if notice is given to the Publisher.

For more information about Heinemann Library books, or to order, please phone
++44 (0)1865 888066, or send a fax to ++44 (0)1865 314091. You can visit our website
at www.heinemann.co.uk.

Any words appearing in the text in bold, **like this**, are explained in the Glossary.

Contents

Introduction

The Olympic Games? You must have heard of them. Spectacular festivals of sport … huge crowds of spectators … lots of ceremonies and processions …, almost everyone knows that much about the Olympic Games. So what else do we know?

Well, only men are allowed to take part in any of the events, and they must be naked. Almost any woman found in the stadium, even just to *watch*, can be executed. On the second day, there are chariot races. On the third, 100 oxen are slaughtered. On the fourth, athletes take part in a combat sport where they are *expected* to break each other's fingers….

Is any of this beginning to sound strange? It should do. The second paragraph describes the *original* Olympic Games – first held, in Greece, more than 2500 years ago. But the first paragraph describes those ancient Games too. Like the modern Olympics, they were fantastically popular sporting occasions – even though, as you can see, there were one or two major differences!

Keeping fit

The Greeks had practical reasons for keeping fit and playing sport. According to the Greek writer Xenophon: 'A good citizen must keep himself in good condition, ready to serve his state at a moment's notice. The instinct of self-preservation demands it likewise: for how helpless is the state of the ill-trained youth in war or in danger! Finally, what a disgrace it is for a man to grow old without ever seeing the beauty and the strength of which his body is capable!'

The opening ceremony of the Olympic Games in Atlanta, USA, in 1996.

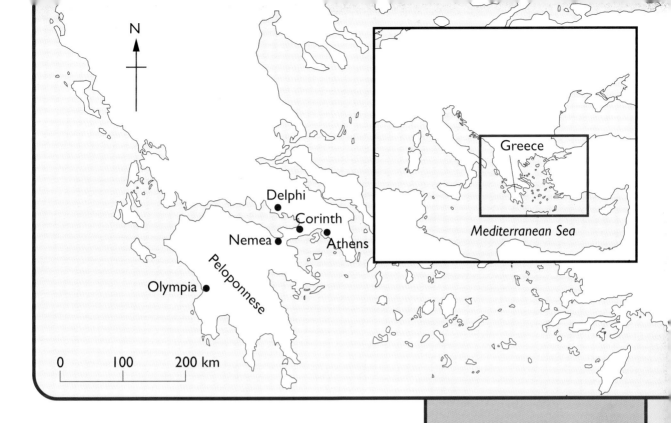

Heroic beginnings

The ancient Games were held every four years at a place called Olympia – to honour the great Greek god Zeus. According to tradition, the first Olympic champion was Coroebus of Elis, a local cook. He won the sprint race in 776BC. By that time, the Games were probably about 500 years old already. (That, at least, is the belief of **archaeologists** who have **excavated** at Olympia; there are no reliable written records.) The ancient Greeks, who loved their **myths** and **legends**, claimed that the hero Hercules was the Games' **founder**.

Olympia was not exactly a *town* in ancient Greece – more like a great sports centre combined with an important place of worship. It lay within the **city state** of Elis, on an area of land known as the Peloponnese. In ancient times Greece was not a single country but a collection of city states which were often fierce rivals.

We do know that, after 776BC, the Games continued for more than 1000 years. On the following pages, you can read about some of the things that happened at Olympia in this very long period of time. As you will see, much of our information comes from books written while the Games were still going on. Other evidence has been dug up by archaeologists. Many of the pictures in this book show statues and vase paintings that were made in ancient times and which give us important evidence about the sports and sportsmen of the ancient Olympic Games.

Only a game?

Many people nowadays take sport very seriously. To them it is almost like a religion. Well, in ancient Greece sport *was* a religion! Athletic festivals, or games, were held as a way of worshipping Zeus and the other gods. The biggest of these festivals was the Olympic Games.

A sporting calendar

In ancient Greece athletic games could be held at funerals, in memory of the dead. They were also arranged as celebrations for heroes. But, above all, they were staged in honour of the gods and goddesses who, the ancient Greeks believed, held people's lives in the palms of their hands.

Greek athletic festivals ranged in size from small contests for local people up to great, regular, national meetings which drew competitors and spectators from far and wide in the ancient world. These national meetings played such an important part in Greek life that people made the period of years from one Games until the next into a unit of time. The four-year period between each Olympic Games was known as an 'Olympiad'. Just imagine if we calculated 20th-century time in the four-year periods between soccer World Cups!

Since the Olympic Games had a religious side to them, a three-month 'Sacred **Truce**' was proclaimed, so that city states which were at war with one another could send their athletes to take part in safety.

No such truce exists for the modern Olympics. In 1916, and again in 1940 and 1944, the Games were not held while World Wars One and Two were raging. In 1924 British athlete Eric Liddell dropped out of the 100 m competition because it meant running on a Sunday which was against *his* – Christian – religion. (But he made up for it by entering the 400 m instead – and winning the gold medal!)

Only a big or rich city could afford its own stadium and the other facilities needed for a major Games. The four top-ranking festivals took place at Olympia (Olympic Games), Delphi (Pythian Games), Corinth (Isthmian Games) and Nemea (Nemean Games).

Eyes on the prizes

The Pythian Games, like the Olympics, were held every four years; the others took place every two years. These 'period Games' were sometimes known as 'Sacred Crown Games'. This was because the winners received only wreaths or crowns to mark their victories. The wreaths at Olympia were made of olive leaves, of laurel plus a handful of apples at Delphi, of pine or sometimes **celeriac** at Corinth and of celeriac at Nemea.

But the athletes at these Games were not pure **amateurs**. When the victors returned to their own **city states**, they were given more practical rewards – like sums of money, which could be very large. Wealthy citizens were often glad to feed and entertain famous victors, and threw big parties for them. An athlete who won at all four major festivals was also given the special Greek title of *periodonikes*, which meant that he was a multiple champion.

Athena, daughter of Zeus, was the guardian goddess of Athens. Its people held games called the *'Panathenaia'* in her honour. Winners and runners-up there were rewarded with very precious prizes of olive oil. The oil was taken from a tree that Athena herself was supposed to have planted.

The ghost stadium

There was no town at Olympia, where the Games took place. Instead there was a holy **sanctuary** and, alongside it, the buildings in which the Games were staged. As you will see later, the ancient Olympics came to an end after the Romans took control of Greece. The whole site of Olympia then fell into disuse, and for 1000 years it was hidden from view by a swamp.

Seeing the site again

During the 19th century, **archaeologists** started trying to **excavate** the old site. A French expedition in 1829 managed to discover the position of the Temple of Zeus there. Then a much longer dig by a German team, between 1875 and 1881, cleared the whole sacred **precinct** and some buildings beyond it. They found the position of the athletics stadium just to the north-east. 20th-century German teams not only excavated the stadium, but restored it as well. This gives modern visitors a really clear picture of the setting of the ancient Games. If they listen hard, they might even hear the ghostly echoes of cheers from 1500 years ago! The noise level back then must have been high. Crowds of over 20,000 – and maybe as large as 40,000 – flocked to watch the sports.

This is how the gateway to the stadium at Olympia looks today. Once it was teeming with people.

Stadium statistics

Archaeologists have shown that, around the middle of the 4th century BC, the stadium was shifted to its present position. The track was surrounded by steep banks of earth on three sides for spectators to sit on. During the Games the spectators slept out in the open. There were no stone seats in the stadium – just a box on the south side where the chief judges sat. Opposite the box was an altar to the goddess Demeter Chamyne. The unmarried priestesses of this goddess were the only women allowed to watch the Games.

The track itself was about 210 metres long and 32 metres wide. It was separated from the spectator areas by a low stone **parapet**. Stone starting lines that were one 'stade' (192.28 metres) apart marked the course at each end. 20 runners at a time could use the track.

The site of Olympia looked like this from above. At the centre is the sacred precinct, known as the *Altis*, or Grove of Zeus. Measuring more than 180 m along each side, it contained the temples of Zeus and Hera (his wife) and other official buildings.

Outside were the stadium itself, the 'hippodrome' where horse-races were held (no trace of this has been found, but a writer called Pausanias described it in detail) and the 'palaestra' where combat sports were practised.

There was also the workshop of Phidias, a famous Athenian sculptor. His great gold-and-ivory statue of Zeus was counted as one of the Seven Wonders of the World. Zeus was shown holding a sceptre in his left hand and a figure of the goddess of victory in his right. The name of this goddess might be familiar to modern sports fans: Nike. Just to the south of the *Altis* stood the *Bouleterion* or council house and a statue of Zeus Horkios (which means 'Zeus who **presides** over oaths'). Here the athletes would take an oath to compete fairly during the contests.

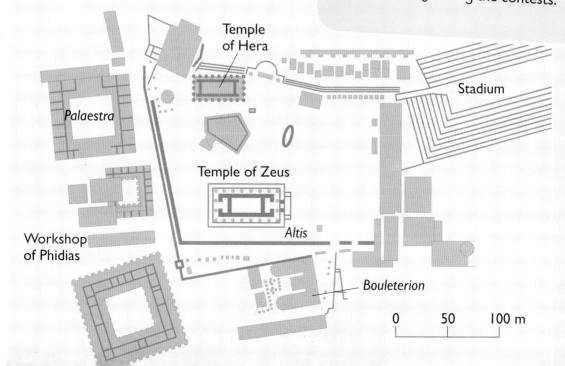

Temple of Hera

Palaestra

Stadium

Temple of Zeus

Workshop of Phidias

Altis

Bouleterion

0   50   100 m

Some days at the races

When we think of the modern Olympics, we often think first of sprinters. This is quite natural. Some of the greatest and most famous athletes of the 20th century have been 100 metres and 200 metres runners. And as a spectator, you do not need to know lots of complicated rules to be thrilled by the sight of the world's fastest men and women racing. But at the Atlanta Olympics in 1996, 26 sports were featured – ranging from **equestrianism** to beach volleyball and from judo to yachting – and within these 26 sports, no fewer than 271 different events were staged.

In ancient times, more and more sports were included in the Olympics too. On page 22 you can see how it grew into a busy five-day festival, but for many years the sole event was the sprint. This took place over a distance of one 'stade' – a single length of the track. In later times other races were added: including the 'diaulos' (two lengths) and the 'dolichos' or long-distance race, which could be run over about four kilometres. There was also a race in full armour, which must have been a sweaty, awkward affair. There were no such problems for runners in the other races: they competed naked!

Running in full armour was more like a novelty race than a serious contest. But it reminded spectators of an original, non-religious reason for the Games – to train up the competitors for war.

Winner takes all?

Nowadays all Olympic runners' performances are timed with great accuracy – although beating their fellow athletes to the gold medal is still the most important thing. At the ancient Games athletes raced only against one another, not against a clock.

To them, all that mattered was the honour and glory of victory — whatever the winning margin. Since 1908, the modern Games' unofficial motto has been this: 'The most important thing in the Olympic Games is not to win but to take part, just as the most important thing in life is not the triumph but the struggle.' Athletes at ancient Olympia would have been baffled by that idea. It also seems to be **alien** to many people involved in sport today. ('It's not the winning' — as an advertisement for one sporting goods manufacturer recently proclaimed — 'it's the taking apart!')

This picture from the 4th century BC shows athletes throwing the discus and javelin.

Field of honour

As well as track events, the stadium spectators could enjoy 'field' sports like jumping — long, but not high — and throwing the discus or the javelin. There was also a five-event contest known as the '**pentathlon**'. The olive-wreath winner of that sport had to run, jump, throw both discus and javelin *and* wrestle. (Since 1912 a modern pentathlon has been included at the 20th-century Olympics. It features shooting, swimming, fencing, riding and running.)

Winning any contest was important, but not winning at all costs. Competitors and officials alike had to take an oath to stick closely to the rules and neither to offer nor take bribes. Cheating of any kind was severely punished — sometimes by special whipping-men who were kept on stand-by. Fines for wrongdoing paid for '*zanes*' (bronze statues of Zeus) to be built. The row of these on display at the entrance to Olympia reminded new arrivals that they were always under the great god's eye. Even that was not enough to stop some cheats from bending the rules, but it seems that foul play and bribery were not common.

Wrestling wonders

Wrestling was extremely popular in ancient Greece. The right way to wrestle was taught at many special schools – and ordinary people as well as **professionals** loved to take part in this very old sport. The best wrestlers of all competed at the Olympic and other Sacred Crown Games. Some of them were so mighty – and so popular with the crowds and with writers – that we still know their feats and names today.

Milo of Kroton

An early Olympic superstar was a wrestler called Milo the Giant, from the Greek **colony** of Kroton in southern Italy. He won at Olympia as a boy, probably in 540BC, and then another five times as an adult. He also won 26 crowns at the other three Sacred Games, over a period of at least 24 years.

Modern wrestlers and boxers must compete in 'classes' depending on their weight. In ancient times there were age divisions but no weight classes. This led to some great feats of eating because the bigger and stronger you were, the better.

According to reports, Milo of Kroton ate 9 kg of meat and 9 kg of bread each day, and washed it down with 10 litres of wine. Once he carried a four-year-old bull around the stadium at Olympia before eating it all in the course of a single day!

Milo could stand on an oiled discus and stay on it, however hard anyone tried to push him off. He was also said to tie a string around his temples, then make the veins there swell up so much that they burst it. And the writer Diodorus Siculus described how he once led his countrymen to victory against a far larger army from Sybaris. Apparently, he came to the battle wearing his Olympic crowns.

As with more modern popular heroes, some of the stories told about Milo seem a little far-fetched. This was how he was supposed to have met his death: while out walking in the countryside, he found a partly split tree, with wedges still stuck into the springy wood. He tried to pull the tree completely apart, but when the wedges fell out, the tree snapped tightly shut on his hands. He could not free himself and, in the end, wolves came and finished him off.

Food for fighting

Astyanax of Miletus, a regular wrestling winner at the Games, was famous for his enormous appetite. Once at a party he was said to have offered to eat everyone's food by himself – then went ahead and did so. After he died, his bones were so big, they did not fit into the large jar in which people's remains used to be buried. His family had to supply a second jar!

Most wrestling scenes in Greek art show the standing part of the bout, rather than ground-fighting – although both were traditional features of the sport. Ancient wrestling could be skilful and scientific. The rules did, however, allow a wrestler to strangle an opponent into submission.

A Sicilian Greek, Leontiskos, won at Olympia in the mid 5th century BC even though he could not throw his opponents. So how did he succeed? He broke their fingers!

Brilliant boxers

Wrestling was just one of the popular 'heavy sports' of ancient Greece. A second – which we also still have today – was boxing. But there were several important differences between the sport then and now. There was no ring, for example, nor was there any point-scoring – you either won or you lost. Bouts went on until one man accepted defeat by holding up a finger or was simply knocked out cold. Sometimes winning came at a high cost: any boxer killed during a contest was proclaimed the victor, while his killer was turned away from the stadium.

Boxing in the blood

Great sporting ability often passes from one generation of a family to the next. This was certainly true of Diagoras of Rhodes (5th century BC), his sons and grandsons. Diagoras' own great-grandfather was a king, but according to the great Greek writer Aristotle he also had the blood of *gods* in his veins: Hermes, the messenger god, was said to have been his father. A man of enormous size and a supreme boxer, he became a '*periodonikes*' by winning at each of the Sacred Crown Games, as well as at many other festivals.

His sons Akousilaos, Damogetos and Dorieus all won Olympic crowns after him. And his daughters Pherenike and Kallipatira each produced sons who went on to win Olympic crowns in their turn. Kallipatira even won fame herself – by becoming one of the few married women who actually saw an Olympics and lived to tell the tale.

This magnificent statue of a boxer was made in the 1st century BC. You can see his hands wrapped in sharp **thongs**, which were the ancient alternative to modern boxing gloves. His face and ear show scars inflicted by someone *else* with similar wrappings!

Find out how she did it on page 24. Six victory statues of Diagoras and his descendants were put on display at Olympia. We know about them because parts of the **inscriptions** on them have survived until today.

Stick to the rules

The Greeks liked to think that boxing was an art. They told a **legend** that, at the first Olympic festival, Apollo – the god of music and art – defeated Ares – the god of war – at boxing. To them, real champions fought with their brains as much as their fists.

A man called Onomastos, from Smyrna, is believed to have drawn up the rules for boxing, some time before 688BC. There were no rounds, and the contest went on until one boxer or other held up a finger to accept defeat – or else was knocked out cold. Another man from the same part of Greece, the stylish Pythagoras of Samos, showed that brains were as important as brute force – triumphing through skill and intelligence. In 588BC he arrived at the Games and applied to box in the boys' division. Laughed at for being too old, he entered the men's division – and won.

But if Olympic boxing still makes you feel squeamish and you do not share the ancient Greeks' belief that it was a thing of beauty – do not turn over and read about another 'heavy sport'. It was not for those of a nervous disposition!

Officials armed with sticks made sure that boxers played it fair and square. Clinching and gripping an opponent's arm were both forbidden. An official might use his stick to remind a competitor of that!

Petrifying pankration

Have you ever heard the expression 'no holds barred'. It means that anything goes – you can use any method you like to achieve your goal. *Pankration* (meaning 'complete strength' or 'complete victory') was an ancient-Olympic combat sport in which almost no holds were barred. Strangleholds, kicking, breaking fingers, dislocating limbs – each of these was used in the attempt to put your opponent down. It was an all-out fight, and the writer Pindar recognized this: 'One must wipe out one's rival by doing everything,' he calmly observed.

Perhaps not surprisingly, *pankration* contests attracted very large crowds of spectators. Champion pankratiasts like Theogenes of Thrace won undying fame. Just as nowadays the winner of the 100 metres sprint is called the Fastest Man on Earth, so the winner of the *pankration* crown could have been called the Strongest (or maybe just the Nastiest!).

One of the immortals

Theogenes of Thrace enjoyed a marvellously successful career as both a boxer and a pankratiast, and after he died he was worshipped as a god. Reports say that he won between 1200 and 1400 festivals, including three Olympic crowns in 480 and 476BC. A statue of him was set up in Thrace, and **legend** tells that one of his old opponents, still bitter about a defeat, came and defaced it. The statue promptly toppled over and crushed him to death!

In Sparta, biting and eye-gouging were allowed, but at national festivals they were forbidden in *pankration*.

Prime pankratiastic qualities

Top pankratiasts tended to be big men. It was said that the first victor, Lygdamis of Syracuse, was a giant who stood on feet 45 centimetres long. Such champions had to be determined as well as strong. There was no time-limit to the exhausting fights except nightfall, so *kartereia* or endurance was a good quality to have. Sometimes it could even be enough to secure a victory:

'I witnessed once in a *pankration* contest,' wrote Philo of Alexandria, 'a man who hurled blows with hands and feet, all of them well-directed, leaving nothing undone that might bring him victory, but who gave up, worn out, and finally left the stadium uncrowned. The man being battered, on the other hand, was compact with solid flesh, ... like a stone or like iron – he didn't give in to the blows and broke the force of his opponent by the toughness of his endurance until he won the final victory.'

Amazingly, though, the Greeks thought boxing was the more dangerous sport. An athlete who wanted to compete in both events at Olympia asked for the *pankration* to be held first, so that he would not come to his second contest already wounded. And according to one belief, if you dreamed about *pankration*, that was a bad omen. But if you dreamed about boxing, that was even worse – because it meant you were going to suffer bodily harm!

This vase painting from about the 5th century BC shows two pankratiasts in combat, closely watched by a judge who is holding a branch.

Horseplay

Equestrian or horse-riding events were introduced into the modern Olympic Games at Paris in 1900. At the Atlanta Games of 1996, there were six separate competitions with gold medals at stake, ranging from the individual three-day event to team **dressage**. In ancient times too, horse sports played a major part in the Games held at Olympia, although the events there were rather different....

This **relief** shows a Roman chariot race.

Hip-hip-hippo!

Way back in time, chariot races were a feature of 'Funeral Games'. These marked the deaths of great Greek men. When festival Games began at Olympia, chariot-racing was included there too. This took place in a different building from the stadium, called the **hippodrome**. (*Hippos* was the Greek word for horse.) If you have ever seen the chariot-race scene in the old film *Ben Hur*, about ancient Rome, you will know how thrilling these races could be. The crowds hit a fever pitch of excitement – not just at the skilful charioteering, but also at the spectacular crashes and pile-ups.

Racing horses were expensive to keep and train – and you needed two or four of them to pull a chariot. Rich horse-owners hired jockeys and charioteers to do the actual racing, which could be extremely dangerous. In the 5th century BC, Damonon of Sparta and his son were successful owners who also occasionally raced themselves. But they were an exception.

Horses for courses

Racing chariots were not like the sturdy vehicles used in ancient warfare. They were lightweight carriages with two big wheels. The drivers stood well back, over the axle, and held the reins in their hands. (In Roman races, the reins were tied behind their backs, so *they* had no way of getting the horse to 'brake'. This meant that the races would be faster but more dangerous.) For a while too, mule-cart racing was popular. Mules are a cross between a horse and a donkey, and were normally used for pulling heavy loads.

The age of the racing animals was important, since there were separate races for full-grown horses and younger 'colts'. Horse judges examined the creatures closely before and after races, and horse-doctors were on call for health problems. And, as in all Olympic sports, there had to be fair play at all times. After a judge called Troilus put in some horses and colts for Olympic competitions, and won in both classes, judges were banned from entering their own animals.

It's my empire and I'll race if I want to

Holders of Olympic crowns were famous far and wide. As ancient Greece fell under the control of Rome, many Romans took a great interest in the Games. The unpredictable Emperor Nero decided to compete himself when he visited Greece in AD67.

First he made the Olympic officials change the date of the whole festival, then he entered a chariot race. He was thrown to the ground and did not complete the course. But the nervous officials gave him the crown anyway – since he surely *would* have won if he had not fallen.

Thus Nero's dream came true: he had won immortality as an Olympic victor. Or had he? When he was dead, the judges at Olympia thought again. They cancelled the festival of AD67 from the records, thus removing Nero's name from the list of winners.

Getting in shape

As you will have gathered by now, sport in ancient Greece was a serious business. Whether you were a runner, combat athlete or charioteer, you could not simply turn up at the Olympic Games and hope for the best. Nor could you easily do another job in between festivals. This was because you had to put in long periods of specialist training, paying particular attention to what you ate and drank. If you then succeeded at the Games, you received the rewards of fortune and fame – ancient Olympic champions were like modern football and movie stars rolled into one.

Ancient Greek sports centres

Combat athletes practised at a *palaestra*. From around the 5th century BC, a bigger sports complex called a *gymnasion* was built in many towns and cities. These places were usually open to the public and included a *palaestra* plus a covered running track, playing fields, baths and an altar for making **sacrifices** to the gods.

This scene from an ancient Greek cup shows what went on in a *palaestra* – a place where combat sports were practised.

The two young men on the left are wrestling, watched by a trainer. He holds a stick, which he would not be afraid to use! On the far right a boxer starts to wrap his hands with **thongs**, while next to him an athlete is using a pickaxe to soften up the ground where he will exercise – there were areas of softened sand and mud for wrestlers to practise on.

Fans liked to come and watch their athletic heroes training, and also to get themselves fit. The ancient Greeks were very keen on physical fitness. They saw the human body as a thing of great beauty, and they believed – as we do – that exercise could improve mental health as well. Sports watchers saw a link between the way an athlete looked and the way he competed. Types popularly known as the 'Eagle', for example, were fierce and strong but might give in when the going got tough. The 'Bear' was slow but difficult to budge.

Whether they were Eagles, Bears or even 'Pieces of String' (sinewy and lithe), athletes preparing for the Olympics would spend months in training to reach the qualifying standard. Then they had to get to Olympia at least a month before the Games began. There they continued to train, watched by local officials who could flog or banish any athletes who did not obey instructions. Then, at last, the Games began. On the next page you can find out just how they were organized.

Trainers and coaches paid close attention to their athletes' diets. Most people ate only barley-bread, fruit, cheese, vegetables and perhaps some fish. Often they got to eat meat only during religious festivals. Top wrestlers, however, gorged on joints of mutton, lamb, **venison** and beef to put on extra weight and muscle.

Without the gifts showered on them by their fans and admirers, many wrestlers could not have afforded so rich a diet. Their meat diet was only part of a strict schedule of rest, exercise – and sometimes a **purging** of the athlete's body by forced vomiting.

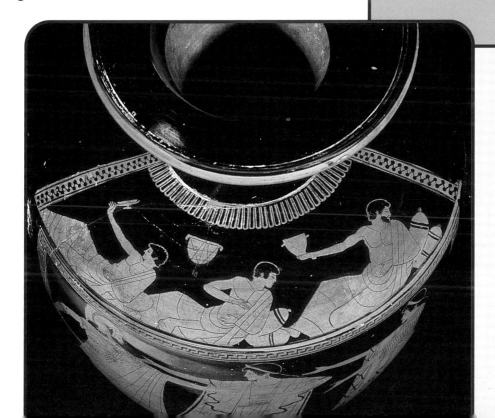

The five-day festival

'If you have worked in a manner worthy of coming to Olympia, and have done nothing in an offhand or base way, proceed with good courage; but as for those who have not so exercised, go away wherever you like.'

Day One

Above are the instructions that were given to athletes, their fathers, brothers and trainers on Day One of the Games. All of them had to swear that they would participate in a fair way. The officials also had to take this oath. And it was up to them to make sure that all the athletes were free-born Greeks (not slaves), and that they had never been accused of **homicide**. Then the competitors entered the stadium and gave their names. In the afternoon the first events took place: running, wrestling and boxing for boys. The Games were on!

Days Two and Three

By the mid 7th century BC, the second day of the Games was a busy one. It featured the **pentathlon** inside the now-packed stadium, and horse-racing and chariot races in the nearby *hippodrome*. It must have been hard to fit all the pentathlon events in. Some historians think that if an athlete easily won the discus, javelin and jump, he was judged to be the overall winner without having to run or wrestle.

The Olympic Games were not just a mixture of religion and sport, but also of sport and war. Nowhere was this clearer than in the javelin event. Athletes threw lighter javelins than those used by soldiers, but they were still basically weapons.

Soldiers and athletes alike sometimes attached a little loop of leather. By putting their first finger into the loop they could throw further and more powerfully.

The jump may have been like our modern triple jump – but with a major difference. Jumpers at Olympia launched themselves into the sandpit holding weights, which they used for gaining extra distance in the swing forward.

On the morning of Day Three, it was the ritual to **sacrifice** 100 oxen in honour of Zeus. (The ash of their burned-up thighs was kept, while the rest of the joints were cooked for a big feast which was held at the end of the Games.) In the afternoon, the running races were held in front of the frenzied stadium crowd. How that crowd must have cheered at the four Games between 164 and 152BC – an all-time great called Leonidas of Rhodes won *three* crowns at each of them.

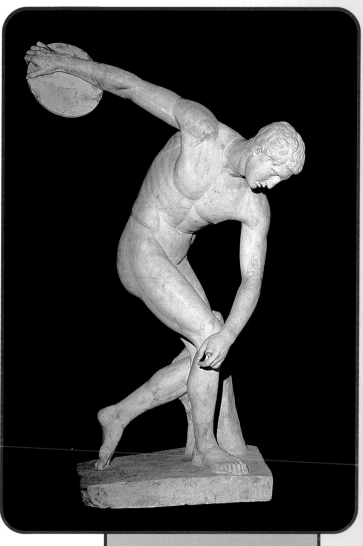

Days Four and Five

One of the events Leonidas excelled at was the race in armour. This was held on Day Four, as well as all the combat sports – wrestling, boxing and *pankration*. Then on Day Five it was time to celebrate. The closing ceremonies included a procession of the winners, followed by their crowning with olive wreaths. After that, it only remained to enjoy the final feast, then go back home and prepare for the next Olympics in four years time!

After the Games, life-sized victory statues of Olympic champions were set up. Unfortunately, very few have survived whole until today – so we have no clear idea what such heroes as Leonidas of Rhodes looked like. But like the image above, the statues would have been wonderful works of art in themselves, showing the athletes' grace and beauty as well as suggesting their great ability.

Women not welcomed

At many sports stadia nowadays, you can hear the loud sound of horns. Fans blow them to help to create an exciting atmosphere. At Olympia you could hear brass blaring too – not from the fans, but from official trumpeters. They gave a blast to signal the start of a race, to call the runners back after a false start and to announce the winners.

It must have been hard to hear them. Many thousands of spectators would have been making their own din. So would the trainers – roaring like modern-day coaches on the sidelines. And so would the athletes themselves: grunting and groaning with all their effort, yelling in triumph or despair.

Nearly all the people making this noise would have been men. Apart from a few priestesses, everyone at the Olympic Games was male. Even women who owned chariots and horses were not allowed to enter the sacred area to watch them compete. Their presence was seen as **sacrilegious** – which could be punished by execution. Yet one brave woman thought it was worth risking life and limb just to see the Games.…

This ancient Greek vase painting shows a soldier blowing a trumpet – as heard at Olympia.

Watch that man!

On page 14 you read about the hugely successful combat-sport family of Diagoras of Rhodes. His daughter Kallipatira grew up hearing all about their Olympic victories – and when the time came for her own son to take part, she could not contain her curiosity. Disguised as a male trainer, she slipped into the stadium.

There, to her great delight, she saw her boy Eukles take the boxing crown. Then her delight became a little *too* great: leaping out to embrace the new champion, she blew her own cover! The officials debated what to do with her – and finally let her off, out of respect for her famous family. But from then on trainers had to be as naked as the athletes – to avoid any more confusion!

Although only men competed in the main Olympic Games, there *were* races for young women at other times. A very old temple to the goddess Hera stood at Olympia. Its officials were in charge of training up girl athletes, who then ran short races in the goddess's honour.

Ancient into modern

Women *did* finally get to take part in the Olympics – but they had to wait until the 20th century. At the Atlanta Games of 1996, 3513 women competed (although there were still more men: 6797). Even so, when the modern Games were founded – in 1896 – women athletes were still kept out. This was just one of many ancient traditions which, at first, were continued into modern times.

But we are jumping too far ahead in time. Before describing how the modern Games came to be started, we must first look at why the ancient Games ended.

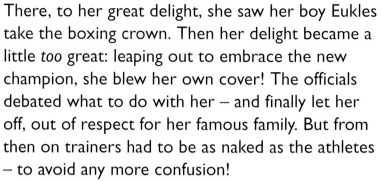

The Games and the Romans

In the middle of the 2ⁿᵈ century BC, Greece became part of the great Roman Empire. The Romans admired many things about the Greek way of life. But they were not so sure about the Greek form of athletics. Roman athletes, for example, usually wore **loincloths** when they trained and competed. They were disgusted to see that the Greeks went naked in public. But the excitement of the Games could not be denied....

More violence please, we're Roman

The Emperor Augustus (27BC–AD14) liked athletic sport, and staged games at Rome in a temporary wooden stadium built near the Circus Maximus. Then the Emperor Nero (AD54–68) was so fascinated by the Greek Games that he actually took part at Olympia (see page 19). By the 4ᵗʰ century AD, more than 150 days each year had been set aside for the million or so people living in Rome to enjoy games. Some of the sport on show – like chariot-racing in the **hippodrome** and horse-racing in the Circus Maximus – followed in the Greek tradition. Some of it, however, did not.

Crowds of over 150,000 people flocked to the great Circus Maximus in Rome and went wild watching four-horse chariot-racing. This picture from the Hollywood film *Ben Hur* shows what a chariot race would have looked like.

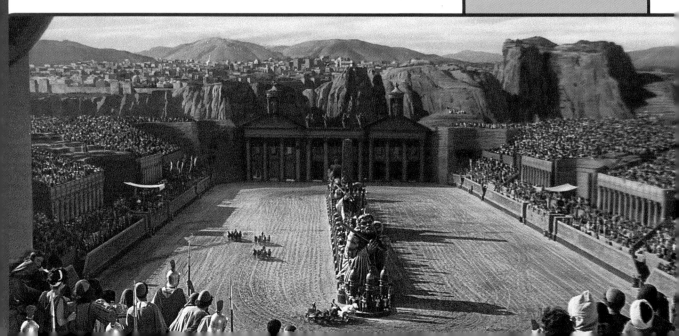

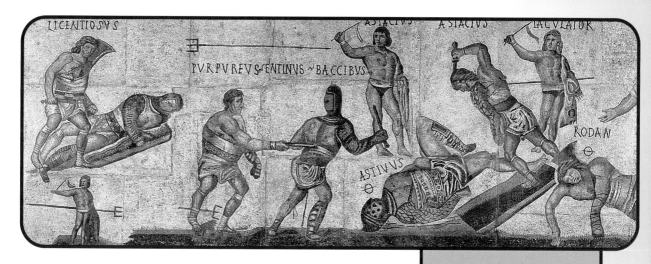

Although the Romans disapproved of public nudity, they had no problem with public violence. In an **amphitheatre** that held 50,000 baying onlookers, animals and humans alike were wounded and killed in so-called 'sporting contests'. The Romans were also keen on the 'heavy sports' they found in Greece: wrestling, boxing and *pankration*. But **track and field** events did not appeal to them so strongly – perhaps because they were too 'tame'!

The Roman public was thrilled by contests between **gladiators**, battles between two armies and their equipment and beast hunts in the arena.

Different strokes for different folks

The Roman view of public sport was really very different from that of the Greeks. The festivals at Olympia were organized, at least in the first place, for the athletes themselves to test their strength, speed or skill against their fellow competitors. Those in Rome were always laid on as **spectacles** for the enjoyment of the public. You could say that, in Greece, sport was mainly about competition. In Rome it was for entertainment.

And there was another big difference between the two views. For the Greeks, sport and religion went hand-in-hand. Greek athletes competed at Olympia, Nemea, Corinth and Delphi as a way of honouring their great gods. For several centuries, the Greeks' open-minded masters in Rome let this continue. But all that changed in the 4th century AD, when Christianity became the Empire's official religion. Early Christians were intolerant of any kind of non-Christian worship – and this was probably why, in AD393, the Emperor Theodosius I abolished the Olympic Games altogether.

De Coubertin's dream

For hundreds of years no one gave a thought to the ancient Olympic Games. The names of the greatest champions were forgotten. Even the site at Olympia no longer conjured up memories of the fabulous old festivals. But during the 1800s a serious new interest in sport began to stir within Europe. In Germany, for example, gymnastics became extremely popular. Two Germans – Johann Guts Muths and Ernst Curtius – even suggested reviving the Olympics. At Much Wenlock in Shropshire, England, a doctor called William Penny Brooks *did* start up some local Games in 1852; and soon afterwards a more national 'Pan-Hellenic' Games began in Greece.

Around 1800 sport began to play a big part in the timetables of private British boys' schools. Favourite sports in Britain, like racing and boxing, were becoming far more organized, and old games like tennis, football and rugby (pictured below) were given brand new sets of rules which everyone had to follow.

Because the British then had a worldwide Empire, they introduced organized sport to the local people wherever they ruled (including future Olympic host countries such as Australia and Canada). But it was a Frenchman – Baron Pierre de Coubertin – who worked hardest to pick up the Olympic Games where the Emperor Theodosius I had forced them to leave off.

A new international era

'Let us export our oarsmen, our runners, our fencers into other lands,' de Coubertin declared in Paris in 1892. 'That is the true Free Trade of the future; and the day it is introduced into Europe, the cause of Peace will have received a new and strong ally. It inspires me to touch upon another step I now propose ... the splendid and **beneficent** task of reviving the Olympic Games.'

After travelling widely in Europe and North America, de Coubertin strongly believed that international sport would be a force for good in the world. At first he found it hard to make other people share his belief. But by 1894 he had won over enough supporters. Plans were laid to stage the first modern Olympic Games in April 1896 – featuring a selection of sports that were popular at that time. And where were they to be held? In Athens – the capital city of Greece, the country that gave birth to the original Olympics.

Victor Duruy, a friend of de Coubertin, once wrote: 'there were splendid festivals, brilliant successes, unforgettable **spectacles**, and at other times vulgarities, disorders, badly arranged ceremonies, and disunited processions.' He was describing the ancient Games – but he could also have been writing about the Games *we* have enjoyed since 1896. When it comes to the Olympics, only one thing is for sure: there is very rarely a dull moment!

Pierre de Coubertin, the 'Father of the Modern Olympics', died in 1937. His heart was buried at Olympia, and this monument was built over it.

Glossary

alien strange or unfamiliar

amateur someone who competes for fun, rather than as a job, and who is unpaid

amphitheatre circular or oval arena with sloping banks of seats rising around a central open space

archaeologist person who studies ancient history, usually by excavating ancient ruins

beneficent worthwhile, helpful

celeriac a kind of celery

city state an ancient Greek city that was also a little independent country

colony place where people move to in order to live in a new country, while still being ruled from their old country

dressage the art of training a horse in obedience

equestrianism riding or performing on horseback

excavate dig up (often ancient ruins)

founder person who starts something up

gladiator trained performer who fights with a sword or other weapon as a form of entertainment

hippodrome course for chariot and horse races

homicide the killing of one human by another

inscription words written on a monument

legend a story which may or may not be true, usually about a hero

loincloth cloth worn around the waist

myth an ancient story, usually about gods and magical events

parapet low wall

pentathlon athletic competition involving five events: running, jumping, wrestling, discus and javelin

precinct enclosed area

preside to control or have authority over

professional paid competitor

purge make clean or clear out

relief a carving that stands out from the surface of a wall or something similar

sacrifice slaughter of an animal as an offering to a god

sacrilegious interfering with something that is sacred

sanctuary a place that is recognized as holy

spectacle great public show

thong strip of leather or animal-hide

track and field sporting events which involve running, jumping, throwing and walking. These include the 100 metres and the javelin

truce the temporary halting of a war or fight

venison meat that comes from deer